TopReaders

# Our Amazing Bodies

Sally Odgers

# Contents

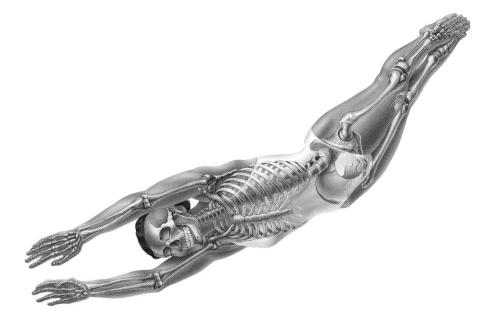

Our bodies are amazing. Every part
has its own special role to play.
Let's find out about our bodies now.

# Cells

Like all living things, our bodies
are made up of millions of tiny cells.
Different cells do different jobs.
For example, blood cells carry  oxygen .

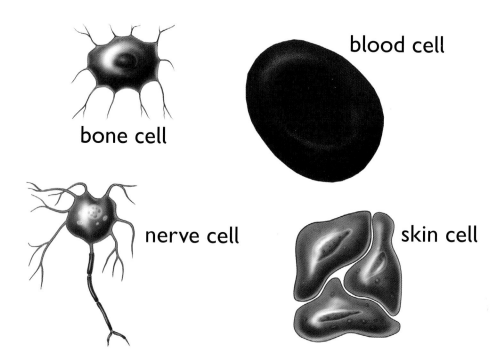

bone cell

blood cell

nerve cell

skin cell

Smaller parts inside our cells do different
things. Each cell is controlled by the nucleus.

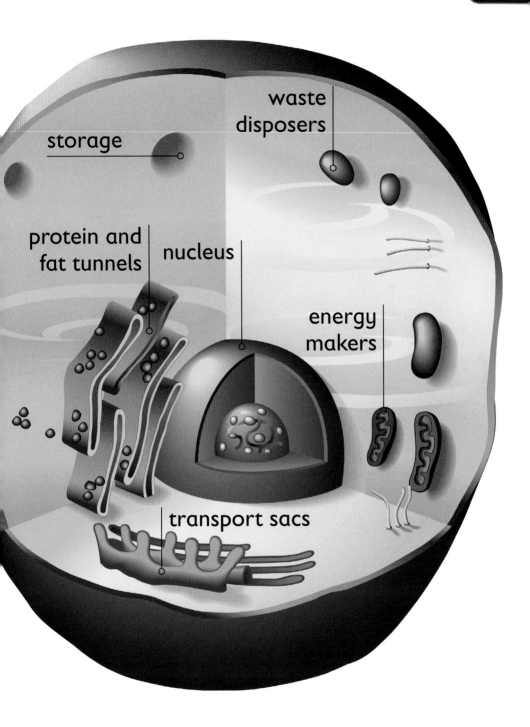

storage

waste disposers

protein and fat tunnels

nucleus

energy makers

transport sacs

# Heart

The heart is the pump that drives our bodies. This strong muscle pumps blood through our arteries and veins.

We can feel our heartbeat from a pulse in each wrist. Use a stopwatch to count how fast the heart beats.

The heart muscle squeezes once every second to pump blood around our bodies.

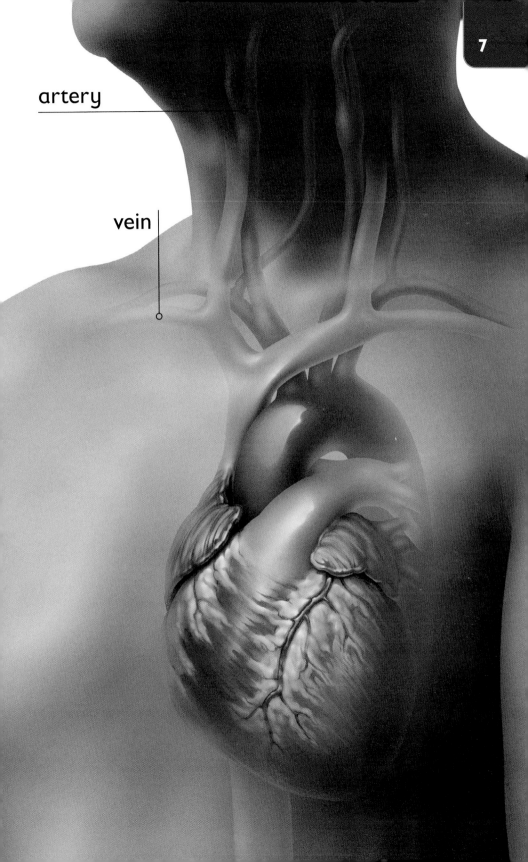

artery

vein

# Lungs

Our bodies need oxygen to live.
Our lungs draw oxygen into
our bodies through the
nose and windpipe.
From there, oxygen
enters our blood.

lung

The heart pumps
blood full of oxygen
around our bodies.

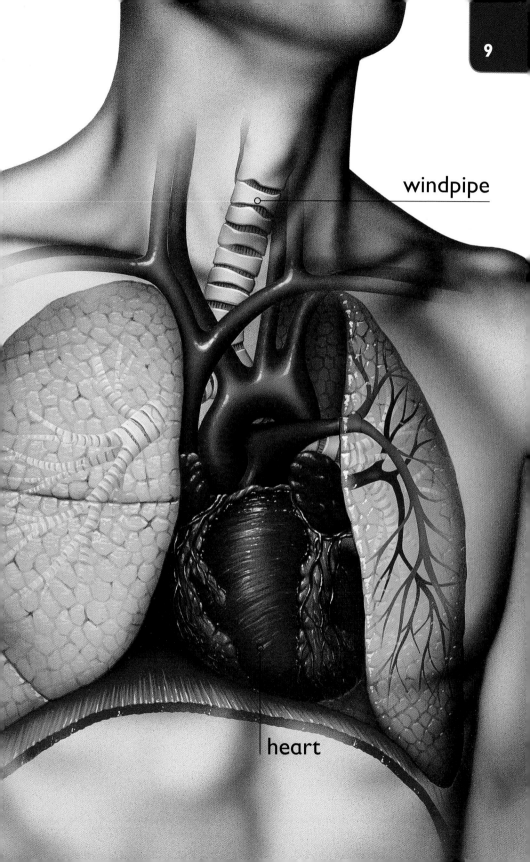

windpipe

heart

# Bones

Our hard bones are the  skeleton
that makes our bodies the right shape.
These bones are strong. They are
many different shapes and sizes.

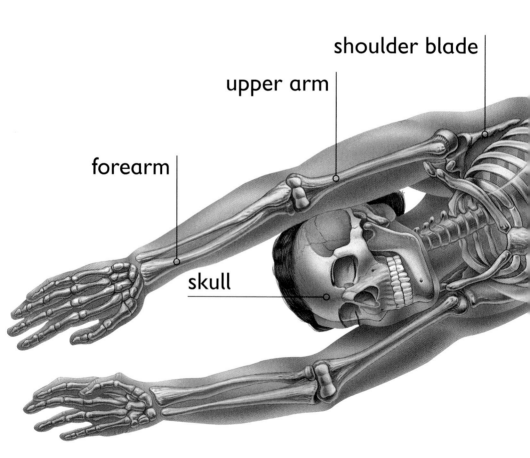

shoulder blade

upper arm

forearm

skull

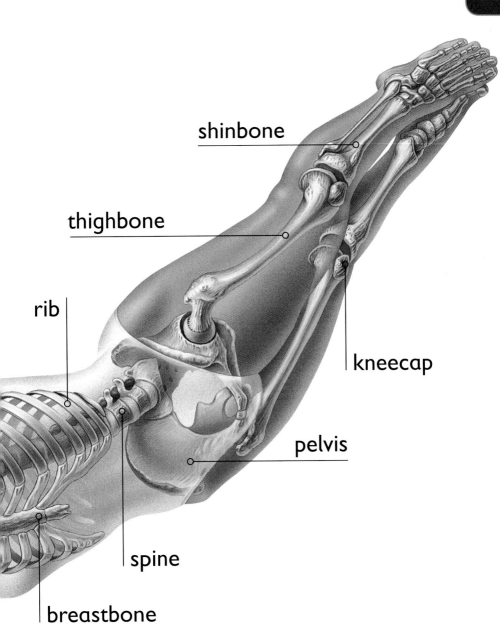

shinbone

thighbone

rib

kneecap

pelvis

spine

breastbone

An adult human has 206 bones.
They fit together like a jigsaw puzzle.

# Muscles

Muscles are made of special tissue .
When a muscle contracts, it bunches
up, and makes part of the body move.

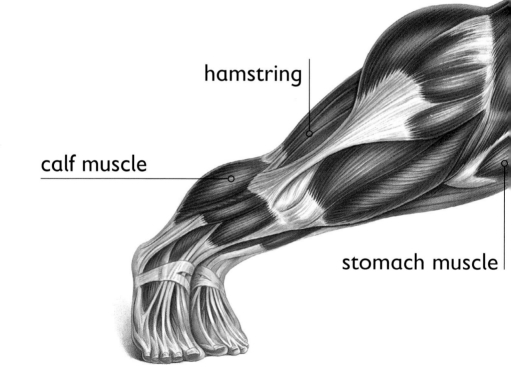

hamstring

calf muscle

stomach muscle

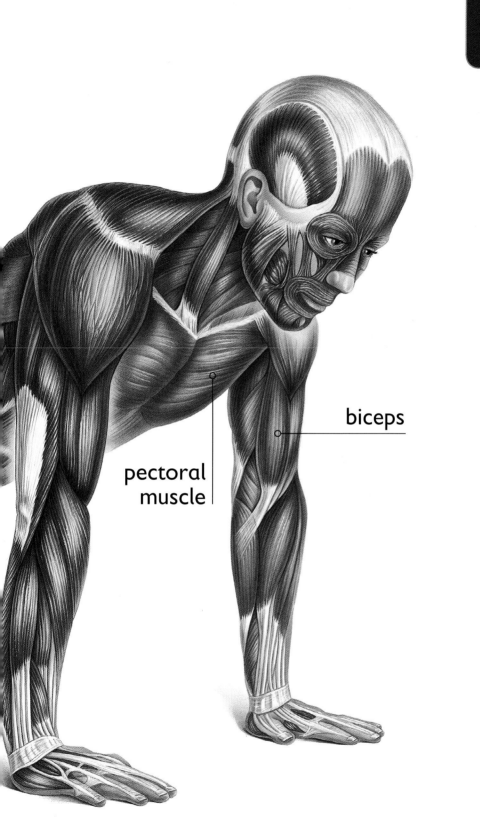

biceps

pectoral
muscle

# Hair and Nails

Hair and nails are made of keratin. We have short hair on our bodies, and longer hair on our heads.

Fingernails can grow very long if you let them.

Nails protect our fingers and toes. We mostly keep our nails clipped short.

long hair

toenail

fingernail

# Teeth

Teeth have different shapes. We bite food with some, and chew with others.

Teeth have  enamel  on the outside and  dentine  inside. They grow out of our jawbones and through our gums.

enamel | dentine

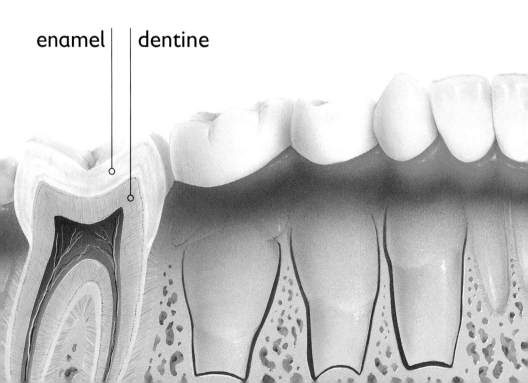

Teeth line the top and bottom jaws. The two sets work together.

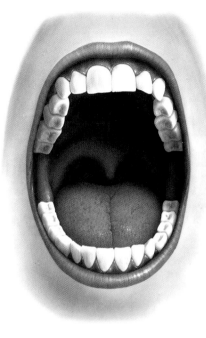

jawbone | gum

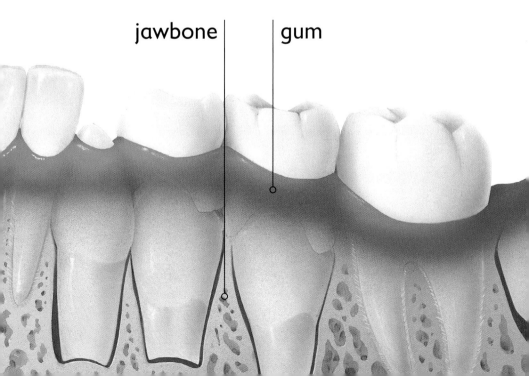

# Eating Food

Food is the fuel for our bodies.
We chew food and swallow it. Then,
our  digestive system  breaks it down.

Digested food gives
us energy, and
builds strong bones
and muscles.

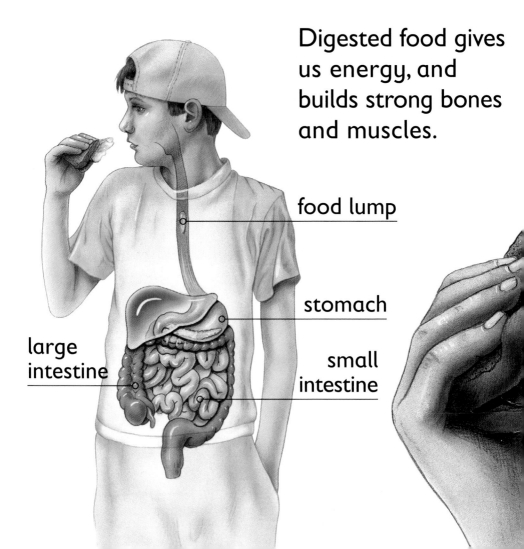

food lump

stomach

large
intestine

small
intestine

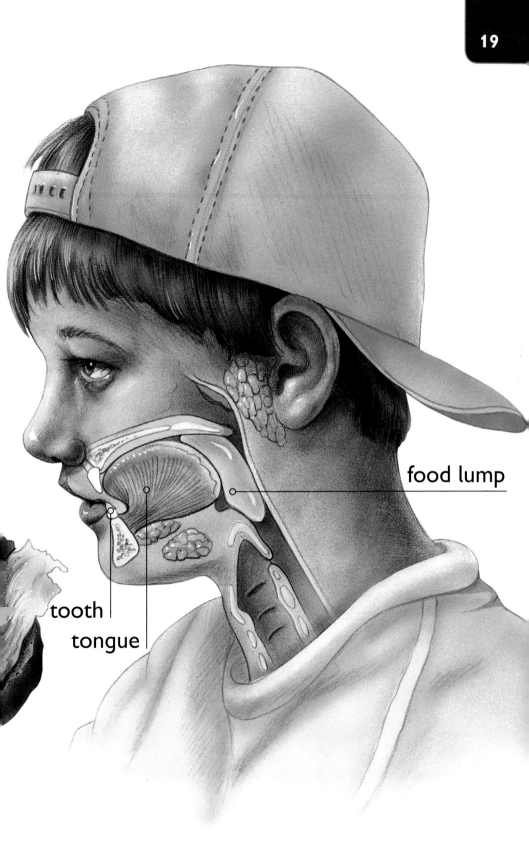

food lump

tooth

tongue

# Brain

The brain tells our bodies what
to do. There are special parts
in the brain for our different
senses, such as sight
and taste.

sight

balance

Our brains work all the time,
even when we sleep.

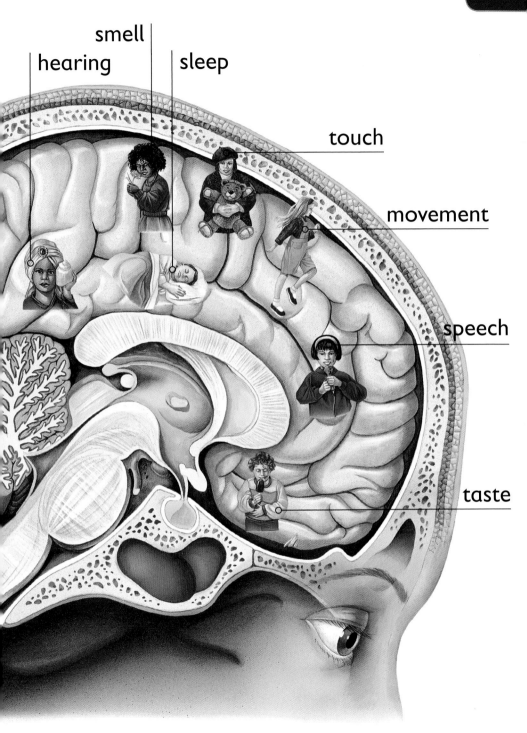

# Eyes

Eyes work with our brains to let us see. They are like windows that connect to the brain.

The dog appears upside down in our eyes.

dog

The brain flips
the image. The dog
then appears the
right way up.

The brain makes us understand
what our eyes see.

Muscles tense, even those in your hair.

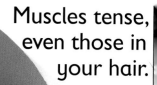

# Danger!

When our brain senses danger, our bodies get ready for action.

Body sweats.

Pupils widen.

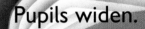

Mouth goes dry.

We might run away.
We might fight.
Either way, our
bodies are ready.

# On the Move

Our bodies need exercise.
Walking and running are good for us.
Swimming is also good exercise.

scuba diving

hang gliding

Some people enjoy
climbing rocks or
hang gliding.

marathon
running

rock climbing

# Bendy Bodies

Our bodies let us bend and stretch. People who are very good at bending can be acrobats.

acrobats using a trampoline

Some people have
very flexible bodies.
If we practice, we
become more flexible.

# Quiz

Can you match each item with its name?

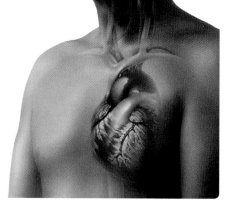

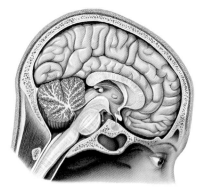

teeth

brain

skin cell

heart

# Glossary

**arteries**: main blood vessels that carry blood from the heart

**dentine**: hard material, similar to bone

**digestive system**: the organs that let us digest, or break down, our food

**enamel**: the shiny hard covering on teeth

**flexible**: bendy

**keratin**: a substance that makes hair, nails, and feathers

**oxygen**: the part of the air we need to breathe

**skeleton**: the set of bones that supports our bodies

**tissue**: a collection of living cells

# Index